GETTING OUT OF DEBT
MADE SIMPLE

Step-By-Step Instructions to Help You Get
Out of Debt and Stay Out of Debt Forever

You Will Learn:

75 Ways To Save Money

How To Save Thousands Of Dollars
Without Increasing Your Income

How to Develop An Effective Family Budget

How To Buy Different Types Of Insurance,
Including Low Or No-Cost Insurance

And Much More

DR. ROSIE MILLIGAN

Professional Publishing House   California

Published and Distributed by:
Professional Publishing House
1425 W. Manchester Blvd., Suite B
Los Angeles, California 90047
www.professionalpublishinghouse.com
Drrosie@aol.com
(323) 750-3592

Cover design: Jay De Vance, III
First printing: August 2012
ISBN: 978-1-8815240-1-4
10 9 8 7 6 5 4 3 2 1

Library of Congress Control Number: 2012946141

In Loving Memory

of my father

SIMON HUNTER

Who often times offered me large sums of money
if I would stop talking for just five minutes.
Needless to say, I never received the money,
for I could never be quiet for that long.

Five whole minutes...No talking!
Are you kidding?

PLEASE NOTE:

This book was written to give you simple guidelines for achieving financial freedom by becoming debt free. It is good practice to be able to manage and control your personal financial affairs before you start spending your life's savings on a business venture.

It is recommended that you consult a financial consultant to help you get off to a great start. Taking an inventory of your spending habits, and comparing it with your income will help you establish a budget for yourself. Setting financial goals will help you achieve financial freedom. Remember, if you don't know where you are going, you might end up where you don't want to be.

ACKNOWLEDGMENTS

I am truly grateful to my friend Barbara Lindsey of Lindsey and Associates for insisting that I write this book. She is a promoter and has been saying for years, "Rosie, you have too much to say, not to say it. I would love to promote you as a speaker, but you have got to get some products." Thank you, Barbara, for pushing excellence.

To my long time friend, Ruby Smith, who has said, "Girl, I see greatness in you." I wish to say thank you for believing in me.

Thanks to my friend, Ernestine Dixon for supporting all my endeavors. I have learned valuable lessons from you about money—your system of budgeting is superb and you always seem to find the money.

I also want to acknowledge my lovely children, Pamela Milligan McGee, M.D., John Milligan, Jr., and Cedric

Milligan, your support and your consideration for what I do have caused me to soar to my highest height.

To my son-in-law, Pastor Kelvin McGee, Thanks for your encouragement and love.

To my grandsons, Jordan Brian McGee, Cedric Milligan, Jr. and Jaylon Dean McGee, I see greatness in you and my expectation from you is to be all that you can be.

I want to acknowledge my sisters and brothers who have considered me their mentor, especially my sister, Clara Hunter King, who shared all of my woes throughout childhood and young adult life. Thanks, Clara. To my baby-sister, Kenyaka, follow your heart and your dreams—build the cultural center that you have dreamed of for many years—God is on your side.

To John Milligan, Sr., my good friend, thanks for sharing your business and computer knowledge with me.

About the Author

Dr. Rosie Milligan, professional business consultant, author, financial/estate planner and Ph.D. in Business Administration, has always been an achiever. Every career or business in which she has been involved includes helping others accomplish their goals in life. Her motto, "Erase No, Step Over Can't and Move Forward With Life," has been a motivating influence for hundreds to whom she has been mentor and role model.

Mother of three entrepreneurs—an M.D., a cosmetologist, and a book and herb store owner—Dr. Milligan lectures nationally on economic empowerment, management diversity in the workplace, and relationships. Her books *Starting a Business Made Simple* and *Getting out of Debt Made Simple*, have helped many across the country. She is the author of seventeen books. She has co-authored four books with her sister, Attorney Clara Hunter King, *What You Need To Know Before You Start A Business, Departing This Life Preparations, How To Write A Book Made Simple, and ABC's On How To Prepare Your Manuscript For Editing, Formatting, And Printing, and What You Need to Know Before You Get Hitched.*

A successful motivational speaker and trainer, she has appeared on numerous television and radio shows, such as Sally Jesse Raphael in New York; A.M. Philadelphia; Evening Exchange in Washington, DC, Marilyn Kagan Show in Los Angeles, and she is a regular guest on Stevie Wonder's KJLH Radio. She is the host of a weekly live Internet talk show and she is founder and director of "Black Writers on Tour.

TABLE OF CONTENTS

- Electricity
- Gas
- Water Bill
- Food
- Automobile
- Gasoline
- Clothing
- Charge Cards/Credit Cards
- School Allowance
- Lunch
- Nails
- Cosmetics
- Telephone
- Special Occasions
- Miscellaneous
- Club Dues & Associations
- Gardner
- Magazines
- Doctor And Dentist

GETTING OUT OF DEBT MADE SIMPLE

Step-By-Step Instructions to Help You Get
Out of Debt and Stay Out of Debt Forever

INTRODUCTION

As a child, I always wanted to know, where I was going, how I was going, who I was going with, what I was going for, and how come, as we said in the south.

You don't know what you've missed by not having a farmer for a father. My father was goal-oriented, and he taught me the same. We were a family of ten, plus whoever else did not have a place to live. My father planned everything to the exact. He planned how many chickens to raise, how many hogs to raise, how many rows of corn to plant, how many rows of watermelons to plant, how many rows of cotton to plant, etc.

I observed other families always running out or being short of something. We always had enough. I asked my daddy, "Why are you so smart?" He told me that God gave us all five senses. Some use some, some use all, and some use none.

My daddy (Simon) considered every possibility when making plans. One day, I asked him, "How do you know how many watermelons to plant each year?" He said, "You've got to know the people."

(Nowadays, we call that, "knowing your market." In those days, the word 'market' meant a store, a place to go buy groceries, etc.)

He said, "You must know that every seed you plant will not produce. The birds and worms will eat some." (Nowadays, the birds and worms are still around eating up what we plant. The birds and worms are the negative people in our lives.)

"I take all those things in account when I am planning. I know how many watermelons my family will eat, how many I will sell, how many I will give away, and how many folks gonna steal from me," Simon said.

I asked him how he knew how much wood to cut and gather for the winter. He said, "You learn by doing. People who don't do nothing, don't learn nothing. I use the same measure for my wood as I do for my watermelon." (Nowadays, we use the term 'same principles' not measure.)

I asked, "Daddy, people don't steal wood, do they?" He answered, "People will steal any and everything." He laughed, and continued. "They will steal *you* if you don't keep up with me." I asked, "Why would they steal me?" He replied, "Everybody wants little smart girls like you." Needless to say, I kept up with Daddy.

Our main source of income came from the cotton fields. One day, I asked my daddy what would happen if enough cotton didn't come up one year. He told me that we needed twenty bales of cotton to be okay. If we came up short, we would finish our crop early, and then we would pick cotton for hire for other people. He always had a back-up plan.

The year prior to my sister entering college, Daddy increased everything he planted.

I was so amazed with Daddy's way of planning. I would often ask myself, "Is this man God? He seems to know everything!" I wanted to be smart like Daddy, so I started seeking knowledge in many areas at a young age. My childhood life inspired me to be a great businesswoman and entrepreneur.

I recognized the importance of being diversified at an early age. Daddy taught me to plan for the future based on my vision, instead of other folks' projections. I did just that. I did not allow the birds and the worms to pluck up my seeds (my vision, dreams, hopes) by saying you are a jack of all trades and a master of none.

CHAPTER I

Financial Food For Thought

The foremost important step in achieving financial freedom is to be crystal clear in your mind as to what financial freedom means to you.

I conducted a survey asking adults and teens what financial freedom meant to them. Below is a list of the responses:

Adult Responses:
- When I can make more money than my wife can spend.

- When my outgoing is less than my incoming.

- When creditors are no longer calling me on the job.

- When I no longer have bills—to be debt free.

- When I can do what I want to do, when I want to do it, and with whom I want to do it.

- When I can work one job and still live comfortable.

- When I can earn enough money to pay my mother-in-law to stay out of my business.

- When I can earn enough money so that my family security does not depend on my wife's income.

- When I don't have to worry about my bills while on vacation.

Teen Responses:

- When my mom and dad are no longer arguing about money.

- When I ask one parent for money, he/she doesn't send me to the other parent.

- When I no longer have to hear from my parents, "Wait until I get paid."

- When parents are able to buy car insurance for teens.

As I listened to all the "whens"—'when this,' and 'when that,'—I asked myself this question, "Who controls the 'whens' and who is in charge of the 'whens'?"

There is a slogan that goes well with this subject…

If it's to be, it's up to me.

Chapter II

Economic Empowerment is Key

You must decide *today* that you are going to control your financial future, regardless of the amount of your income. *Today* is a key word, because most people tend to continue putting off until tomorrow. *Being debt free comes by planning and not by chance.*

Goal setting, planning, and effective means of evaluation are the blue prints for becoming debt free. Below is a list of reasons clients give as to why they cannot set goals and make plans:

- I never know what my husband or wife is going to do.

- My wife or husband is so unpredictable.

- It's hard to plan because my job is shaky.

- We will decide what we are going to do in life when the children are grown and gone.

- How can you plan when every time you look up, some unforeseen expense comes up? For example, car repair, dentist, doctor, etc.

- John is a senior this year; I don't know if he's going to college or going to work

Written goals and plans are very, very important. It is almost impossible to succeed without written goals and plans. In order to become debt free and to achieve financial freedom, it must be a family team effort. Every family member has to know what each member wants, when they want it, and what each member can do to help each other to achieve their goals.

The single or unmarried person should not only be concerned about their goals, but should also be concerned about the goals and plans of the significant person in their life.

I feel so strongly about goals and plans that I would suggest you ask to see the written goals and plans of the significant person in your life. The person should have written goals and plans for the next twelve months, the next two years, and the next five years. You should re-evaluate your relationship with any person who does not have goals and plans for at least the next five years.

I conducted a survey using five hundred people, men and women, with salaries ranging from $800 to $5,000 per month. Eighty-five percent of those surveyed had one thing in common—they had less than $250 saved. Those who earned less than $2,000 per month had the most saved. The amount of income you have today is not the controlling factor that determines your financial freedom. The keys that open the door to financial freedom are: ***Goal Setting, Plans, Evaluation, Re-evaluation, and Commitment.***

GOAL SETTING SCALE

Over the years, I have observed the goal setting and planning patterns of many people. Some people believe the first thing one should do is prepare a family budget, listing all income for the home and all home expenses and then set goals and plans based on what is coming in and going out.

I believe you should look beyond what you see, and what you have today. Goals should be set based on where you see yourself in the future. You must have a larger vision of yourself in order to move out of your comfort zone. One should develop a holistic approach toward goals. Frequently, I ask people, "What are your goals?" Below is a list of responses:

- I want to own my own home one day.

- I want to buy that dream house.

- I want to buy a Mercedes.

- I want to have a home for abused children.

- I would like to build housing for the homeless.

- I would like to have my own business.

It seems as though when we think of goals, we think mostly about the material aspect only. Below is a list of eight areas we must focus on because each impact our financial status:

- PERSONAL

- MENTAL

- FAMILY

- SPIRITUAL

- CAREER

- SOCIAL

- FINANCIAL

- PHYSICAL

It is important for each family member to set a goal for each area above.

BEGIN WORKING NOW!

Be specific about your goals. It is not good enough to say, "I want a home one day." You should write down where you want the house, how many bedrooms, how many bathrooms, the amount you want to pay for it, and the date or month you want to buy it. You should examine your reasons for wanting what you want, the obstacles you will have to overcome, connecting with people who will help you achieve your goal, the skills necessary, and most important, the specific plan of action it will take to reach your goals.

Remember, you may have to give up something in order to reach your goal. Have family members give their input when giving up something that involves the family. Make it a family project. Family members will cooperate more when they feel a part of the project.

LET'S GET THE SHOW ON THE ROAD!

1. Study your GOAL SETTING SCALE and place a check mark by the area of concern.

2. On the MY GOALS worksheet, write down where you see yourself in the next twelve months, the next two years and the next five years in the areas that you have concerns about from your GOAL SETTING SCALE.

3. Complete the GOAL SETTING WORKSHEET, which includes goals that you want to accomplish, the reasons you want to reach these goals, etc.

THE EXERCISES BELOW ARE VITAL TO YOUR SUCCESS OF BECOMING DEBT FREE

On the following pages, you will find the GOAL SETTING SCALE. Place a check mark by the things that you feel that you need to do to make you a better you. Write your plan for the eight areas for your life and where you see yourself within the next twelve months. This is the work that goes with your faith of becoming successful in being debt free

These exercises will help you to see your weaknesses and your strengths, and from this exercise you will be able to put the pieces in the puzzle to your life. Take the time and do the exercises. YOU PROBABLY HAVE MORE TIME THAN YOU HAVE MONEY. SO JUST DO IT.

GOAL SETTING SCALE

Personal

_____   Things that are for me only

Mental

_____   Improve attitude
_____   Enhance intelligence
_____   Seek continuing education and training
_____   Attend workshops and seminars
_____   Purchase tapes and books
_____   Increase enthusiasm
_____   Improve self-image

Family

_____   Improve family relationship
_____   Eat meals together
_____   Spend time together
_____   Improve listening skills
_____   Develop a forgiving attitude
_____   Be aware of tone when communicating
_____   Help build self-esteem of others
_____   Become a good role model
_____   Become principled, but flexible in disciplining
_____   Develop strategy for conflict resolution

Spiritual

_____ Strengthen belief in god
_____ Strive for inner peace
_____ Be a good influence on others
_____ Improve spouse relationship
_____ Become more involved in church
_____ Seek purpose for my life
_____ Improve attitude toward giving
_____ Attend christian education classes
_____ Work on sharing with others

Career

_____ Discover how I feel about what I do
_____ Understand my job
_____ Like my business
_____ Improve relationships with co-worker or employees
_____ Increase productivity
_____ Seek opportunity for job advancement
_____ Seek opportunity for business expansion
_____ Prepare for career transition
_____ Understand company goals

Social

_____	Develop self-confidence
_____	Become more at Ease at gatherings
_____	Work on being friendly
_____	Be more courteous nature
_____	Improve listening habits
_____	Develop Sense of humor
_____	Praise of others
_____	Get involved in community activities
_____	Avoid gossip
_____	Be more positive
_____	Practice good personal hygiene

Financial

_____	Evaluate earnings
_____	living within income
_____	set a personal budget
_____	Place proper priority
_____	Increase savings
_____	Prepare financial statement
_____	Make investment
_____	Stop excessive impulse purchasing
_____	Cease using charge accounts
_____	Assess insurance needs

Physical

_____ Improve appearance
_____ Assess energy level
_____ Plan recreational activities
_____ Participate in regular fitness program
_____ Schedule regular medical and dental check-up
_____ Manage stress control
_____ Plan a healthy diet and nutrition program
_____ Manage weight control

Sexual

_____ Explore my body
_____ Express my sexual needs
_____ Share past experiences that are not conducive
to healthy sex

MY GOALS

My plans, where I want to be, what I want to have, and where I see myself within the next twelve months.

I.   PERSONAL

II.   MENTAL

III.   FAMILY

IV.   SPIRITUAL

V.   CAREER
    (a)   Employment
    (b)   Vocation
    (c)   Business

VI.   SOCIAL

VII.   FINANCIAL

VIII. PHYSICAL

MY GOALS

My plans, where I want to be, what I want to have, and where I see myself within the next two years.

I.   PERSONAL

II.   MENTAL

III.   FAMILY

IV.   SPIRITUAL

V.   CAREER
     (a)   Employment
     (b)   Vocation
     (c)   Business

VI.   SOCIAL

VII.   FINANCIAL

VIII.   PHYSICAL

MY GOALS

My plans, where I want to be, what I want to have, and where I see myself within the next five years.

I.   PERSONAL

II.   MENTAL

III. FAMILY

IV.   SPIRITUAL

V.   CAREER
      (a)   Employment
      (b)   Vocation
      (c)   Business

VI.   SOCIAL

VII. FINANCIAL

VIII. PHYSICAL

GOAL SETTING WORKSHEET

THE SPECIFIC GOAL I WANT TO ACCOMPLISH IS:

_____

_____

_____

_____

_____

THE REASONS I WANT TO REACH THIS GOAL ARE:

_____

_____

_____

_____

_____

THE OBSTACLES I WILL HAVE TO OVERCOME TO REACH THIS GOAL ARE:

_____

_____

_____

_____

_____

THE PEOPLE, GROUPS AND ORGANIZATIONS
I NEED TO WORK WITH IN ORDER TO REACH
THIS GOAL ARE:

_____

_____

_____

_____

_____

THE KNOWLEDGE AND EDUCATION I NEED TO
REACH THIS GOAL ARE:

_____

_____

_____

_____

_____

THE SPECIFIC PLAN OF ACTION I WILL TAKE IN
ORDER TO REACH THIS GOAL IS:

_____

_____

_____

_____

_____

NOW IT'S TIME TO DO THE WORK FOR REAL.

Now that you have finished your project, have each family member to do the same. Once the entire family has completed the project schedule, set aside some uninterrupted time to discuss the project.

It's now getting to be fun. The family is getting to know each other "real good." It's such a good feeling to know that each family member plays an important role in helping to achieve the family goals and financial freedom.

CHAPTER III

Family Budgeting Made Fun

Now that you have set your goals, you know how much money is needed for the projects, and when the monies are needed, let's start taking inventory. Remember, there are no more secrets. If a past due notice comes in the mail, its everybody's business. When you are pressured financially, don't carry the burden alone. It is much easier when you share it. You will be surprised to know that family members have the solution to many of your problems that cause so much stress and pain, if you would only let them be a part.

You are probably thinking that you don't want your problems to become your wife/husband's or children's problems. Your family can appreciate you more when they know why your behavior is abnormal. Whether you want to admit it or not—w burdened with bills, your outgoing is more than your incoming, creditors are calling at home and work—your behavior becomes a little strange.

Start taking inventory by going through your checkbook to see where your money is going. Make a list, and call it Where Did My Money Go?. Make two columns. In the right column, list all bills, house expenses, personal, and miscellaneous, etc. In the left column list all the interest paid for the month. To find the interest, look on your mortgage statement and your monthly bills statements. It is so important to look at the amount of interest paid every month. If you look at it every month, you will quickly decide to take some constructive actions. Make a list of all income for the household with three columns: Depending Monies, Sometimes Monies, and Miscellaneous Monies. Include money from each family member. Look at what you *must* give up, not what you *want* to give up.

Here comes the fun. Each family member will make a dream list. It's so much fun to know what every family member is dreaming. The first dream list you will complete is: Money Is No Object. Now that you have had lots of fun dreaming, go on to complete a Dream List where Money *IS* An Object

The next two pages are your Dream List pages. Complete and have each family member do the same.

You should know that your dreams and goals should not change based on your current financial condition. Your present financial staus is no reflection of your financial future.

MY DREAM LIST

WHERE DO I SEE MYSELF IN THE NEXT TWELVE MONTHS, IF MONEY WAS NOT AN OBJECT?

_____

_____

_____

_____

_____

_____

_____

_____

_____

_____

_____

_____

_____

MY DREAM LIST

WHERE DO I SEE MYSELF IN TWELVE MONTHS, IF MONEY IS AN OBJECT?

_____

_____

_____

_____

_____

_____

_____

_____

_____

_____

_____

_____

MY DREAM LIST

WHERE DO I SEE MY SELF IN THE NEXT TWELVE MONTHS CONSIDERING MY PRESENT FINANCIAL STATUS?

_____

_____

_____

_____

_____

_____

_____

_____

_____

_____

_____

A budget is important no matter how small your income may be.

It is good practice to do an annual (yearly) budget in December for the upcoming year. You should do a monthly budget first. Every month will be different, because some expenses occur on a seasonal basis. Example: birthdays, special occasions, graduations, proms, Christmas, weddings, vacations, tuitions, etc.

A planned monthly budget gives you foresight instead of hindsight. The monthly budget in this book covers most expenses that will occur in any given month. Each month's budget should take into consideration family goals and dream lists. The next few pages will give a guideline for a Family Monthly Budget.

MONTHLY BUDGET

Net Wages After Taxes $ _____

Other Income   _____

_____

TOTAL INCOME $ _____

EXPENSES:

Rent/Mortgage   _____

Electric & Water Co.   _____

Gas Co.   _____

Telephone   _____

Cell Phone   _____

Over-the limit charges
    on cell phone   _____

Information charges from
    telephone operator   _____

Groceries
    Food items   _____
    Non-food items   _____

Insurance
    Life   _____
    Health (medical)   _____
    Disability   _____

Long-Term
    Auto   _____
    Home   _____
Automobile
    Payment or lease   _____
    Gas, oil, etc.   _____
    Maintenance   _____
Childcare   _____
Installment Payment
    Credit Cards   _____
    Installment Loans   _____
    Educational Loans   _____
Clothing
    Purchase   _____
    Laundry   _____
    Pampers or Diapers   _____
    Dry Cleaning   _____
Recreation & Entertainment
    Events   _____
    Dining out   _____
    Lunch at work   _____
    Vacations   _____
    Video rentals   _____
    Gyms & spas   _____
Education
    Tuition   _____
    Books & Tapes   _____
    Seminars   _____

Organizational
    Dues   _____
    Subscriptions   _____

Church
    Tithes   _____
    Offering   _____
    Special Events   _____
    Uniforms, etc.   _____

Personal Care
    Routine Dr. visits   _____
    Physical   _____
    Dentist   _____
    Hair Care   _____
    Nails   _____
    Cosmetics   _____

Bottle Water   _____
Gardener   _____
Bus pass   _____
Children's school allowance   _____

Special Occasions
    Christmas gifts   _____
    Birthdays   _____
    Mother's Day   _____
    Father's Day   _____
    Bridal Showers/Wedding Gifts   _____
    Graduations   _____

Proms   _____
Class ring   _____
School jacket   _____

Miscellaneous
    Banquet tickets   _____
    Raffle tickets   _____
    BBQ Dinners   _____
    Candy drives   _____
    Patron list   _____

TOTAL EXPENSES $ _____

AVERAGE/SHORTAGE $ _____

Once the family budget is completed, it is not enough to just say, "Here it is." Each family member must be willing to make changes. To achieve financial freedom, each family member must make a commitment to the project.

If you want conditions to change in your life, you must change. Remember, if you keep on doing what you have been doing, you will keep on getting what you have been getting. The following page is a commitment for you and your family members to complete. When each member has completed this worksheet, schedule a time to discuss each commitment.

MY COMMITMENT

"I know that if I keep on doing what I have been doing, I will keep on getting what I've been getting."

Things I will do to help cut down on expenses and to help save money.

My contributions to project...

1.

2.

3.

4.

5.

6.

7.

8.

9.

10.

CONGRATULATIONS!

You have completed a great accomplishment. Now, you have the most important job left to do—see if what you've been doing is working for you. It's evaluation time!

You and each family member must complete a monthly evaluation form. You should schedule a time for family discussion.

The evaluation gives you a chance to modify plans and goals, if necessary. You might need to make your twelve-month goals, two-year goals, etc.

The following page is a Monthly Progress Evaluation Form.

MONTHLY PROGRESS
EVALUATION FORM

- I did all things I said I would do to help.

- I did some of the things I said I would do to help.

- I did more than what I said I would do to help.

- I see where I can do much more to help.

List the results you can see, at this point, from your team effort.

List additional things you will do next month to help.

How much money did the family some from my efforts?

CHAPTER IV

75 Ways to Save Money Owning A Business

A business of your own is still the best way to help you keep more of your money in your pocket. I am not talking about taking a hobby and using it for a business, with no intentions of making money. The IRS may be skeptical if you declare a hobby-like activity, such as coin collecting, as a business.

If you are challenged by the IRS, and you fail to prove a profit motive, you could lose all of your deductions retroactive.

This is why it is a smart move for anyone to turn a hobby into a profitable venture. When in business for yourself, you can claim every deduction that any major corporation can claim as a deduction on your income taxes. Your automobile expenses can be used as a tax-deductible expense.

On your personal taxes, you may deduct that portion of your medical insurance that exceeds 7.5% of your adjusted gross income; however, you may deduct 100% of your medical expenses.

As the owner of your own business, you can hire your children. Hiring your child is a win-win situation. You are giving them money anyway—this way they can work for it. Working gives the child a sense of pride and keeps more of what would be tax dollars in your pocket. You can deduct medical expenses for your spouse as an employee.

You can pay your child the amount allowed for standard deduction for that particular year and still claim that child as a dependent. The child can file his/her taxes also and not claim him/herself as a dependent and still owe no taxes. Consult your tax consultant regarding the standard deduction for the year that you have concerns about.

If you have a room in your home that's used exclusively for business activity, then you may deduct a portion of mortgage interest, utilities, telephone and home insurance on your business taxes. You may also depreciate a portion of your home as related to square footage percentage use for the business. You may deduct personal computers and adding machines as depreciable items. You may depreciate that portion of your home use for business. Also you can deduct depreciation expenses on your equipment, even though you do not deduct office use of your home.

AUTO INSURANCE

Consumers could save a substantial amount of money on their automobile insurance policies if they would only pay for the coverage they need.

Coverage needed is liability, comprehensive and collision. Liability has two categories: Bodily Injury, which covers injury to other people, and Property Damage, which covers damage to other people's properties. Comprehensive pays for damages due to fire, theft, etc. Collision covers damages to your automobile when involved in an accident with another automobile or object.

Coverage you don't really need are no-fault, which covers medical, funeral expenses, and work loss. Medical payments cover medical bills and funeral expenses. Uninsured Motorist covers medical and funeral expenses caused by an under insured motorist or a non-insured motorist. Emergency Road Service covers towing of an automobile, and Car Rental Expense covers rental car expenses when your car is damaged.

Please note this information is given as a guide to saving money; however, each person's circumstances are different. You should consult with your business consultant and insurance department for a clearer understanding of what you are doing before dropping certain insurance coverage. Example: Medical coverage—if you have personal medical insurance coverage, your medical insurance will pay for your medical expenses incurred. Why pay for duplicate benefits? There cannot be duplication of payments for medical expenses or losses under vehicle insurance and personal insurance.

What if you have medical coverage provided by your employer, you quit or are terminated, you do not or cannot afford to convert your medical insurance policy, and, meanwhile, you are involved in an accident and suffer injury? Can you see why much consideration should be given when deciding on any insurance coverage?

It is good practice to increase your deductible to a minimum of $500 to $1000. Most people will not report damage under $500 for fear of policy increase, so why pay more for a lesser deductible.

If your car is not worth very much, you may consider not carrying comprehension and collision depending on the price for the coverage. Again, weigh the circumstances. If your car is stolen or totaled due to an accident, you will receive no insurance compensation. When purchasing insurance, ask about available discounts, such as:

1. Good Driver

2. Alarm System

3. Multi Automobiles

4. Senior Citizen Discount

5. Driving Training Class Taken

AUTO INSURANCE FOR TEENS

Let's look at auto insurance for teens. Insurance coverage for teens is outrageously expensive. It is no longer a luxury for a teen to drive an automobile, it has become a necessity. Many teens work after school, and on weekends to help support themselves, their parents and siblings. Many teens work nights or late evening hours. Because of the street violence today, teens are in danger just sitting at bus stops.

For economic purposes, a parent should buy a used car for a teenager. The car should be registered in the child's name, obtain the bare minimum liability required by law on the automobile. In many cases, the insurance can be as much as the car note. (Buyer, be aware!)

LIFE INSURANCE

One must ask this question when considering life insurance: Do I need it? Lots of people don't.

If you decide that you do need life insurance, you need to choose between a term policy (death benefit only) and a form of permanent, or cash value policy, which combines death protection with a savings or investment plan.

When shopping for life insurance, you must come to grips with how much coverage you need and for how long you will need that amount of coverage. Your age, family responsibilities, health, income, assets, investments, employers benefit, number of children, children's age, children's goals, children's health and social security benefits, should all be taken into consideration when deciding the amount of coverage you need.

Have your insurance agent give you a comparison price for a specific amount of life protection for term and permanent (whole life). After examining the cash build up in a whole life policy, you must decide if you can make more money for yourself if you buy term and invest the difference or can the insurance company make more money for you. The other questions you might ask are: Why am I buying insurance? Is it a specific amount of death protection I want for my family? Is it savings or investment that I want?

You should write these questions down and keep them handy when the insurance agent is there for the appointment. Sometimes, if you are not careful, an insurance agent will pull you away from your agenda, and you will wind up on his/her agenda.

SCENARIO

A simple guideline to help you determine the amount of life insurance you might want to have:

Example 1:

You own a home and no other assets or investment. You owe $124,000 on your home. You have a son 16 years of age. Your son is in the 11th grade. He has two more years in high school. He plans to go to college for a Master of Business Administration, which should take five to six years of college. Your son will have no support from father or other family members. If you died today, how much insurance would you want to have?

***Example 2*:**

You are divorced and the whereabouts of the children's father is unknown. You own your home, and you owe $124,000. You have no other assets or investments. You have a son who is 16 years old. He is in the 11th grade. He has two more years in high school. He plans to go to college for a Master of Business Administration, which should take approximately five to six years. You have two older children: a son who is 23 and owns a barber shop; and a daughter who is 25 years old. She is married. If you died today, how much life insurance would you want to have?

LET'S TAKE A LOOK AT A LOW OR NO-COST INSURANCE

TODAY'S NEW *HYBRID* PLANS

The below information was provided by Christopher Hawk, an author of financial literacy publications and a financial advisor of 22 years. He may be reached at (310) 391-8086 between 10am to 5pm PST.

Low or **No-Cost Insurance**
Today's new hybrid plans

When you think of insurance in any form, thoughts of *never ending premium payments* coupled with *no returns* come to mind. However, for savvy shoppers who don't mind taking in a little consumer education, both better and maximum benefits may be obtained for *your hard earned money*.

Such is the case when it comes to disability, long term care and life insurance available today, throughout the United States of America.

Today's plans now offer various **Return of Premium** options or *early liquidation* benefits.

Depending on the regulatory language approved by your state, terms such as Return of Premium, Endowment Rider, Accelerated Benefits, Terminal Illness, Chronic Care riders, etc. may be used.

Because each company does business differently and offer services differently, *your money back options* may be represented as a small percentage of your total premiums over the years of coverage; or, **100%** of *your money back.*

Early liquidation of traditional life insurance means... the *spending down* of the beneficiary's death benefits (proceeds) before you die; for your own personal use *as you deem* appropriate.

Example:
A person has $100,000 life insurance policy, and is diagnosed as having cancer; the person may not have enough medical insurance, or worse—no insurance at all.

The policy holder may elect to liquidate their life insurance death benefit before dying; assuming they have one of today's hybrid plans.

At **2% - 4% *per month*,** they may conceivably receive monthly checks up to **$4,000,** or up to policy's pre-set maximums.

Some plan riders are extra benefits and may not affect the base policy benefits or death proceeds.

The beauty of today's hybrids plans is that they may offer benefits with respect to long term care, disability or life insurance.

As an added bonus, today's plans may also be ***tax-deferred*** or ***tax-free income*** should early liquidation fall under the IRS's category of ***"Qualified Health Expenses."***

Though hybrid plans are not meant to replace traditional separate plans, they may help to address multiple needs or concerns for both *individuals* and *small businesses* that operate on tight budgets.

Finally, when structured or used correctly, the *return of premium* options may also be used to supplement your income on a tax-advantaged basis during *your retirement years*.

HOME INSURANCE

Increase your deductible to $500.00 on your homeowner's policy. Have your agent explain the additional costs for each additional coverage, other than liability, theft, and fire?. Then and only then, can you decide if it is worth the cost. Don't buy flood or earthquake insurance unless you are in a designated flood or earthquake zone. Keep purchase receipts for home items such as furniture and appliances, expensive jewelry and furs, cameras and video equipment. It is important when there is a loss.

Re-evaluate and update your insurance as you increase your assets. You may need to purchase a special coverage for expensive personal items. Make sure you have full knowledge as to your basic policy limits on theft and damage of personal items.

TENANT'S POLICY

If you are renting a house or apartment, you should purchase a tenant insurance policy. Tenant policies cover household contents, personal items, and additional living expenses.

LANDLORDS

If you are a landlord, make sure your properties are covered with proper liability insurance. The risks are too great not to be covered.

MEDICAL INSURANCE

Medical insurance is very expensive, especially when it covers doctor's visits, etc. Most families cannot afford the luxury of all those choice benefits. You mainly need a policy that covers major medical. Major medical covers large risk, like hospitalization and catastrophic illness, etc. If you fail to insure yourself against catastrophic illness, your assets can soon be eaten up by medical bills. Remember, most people will spend all they have to feel better. The higher your deductible, the less you pay for medical coverage. Consider $5,000 or more deductible if you have liquid assets available.

DISABILITY INSURANCE

If you find the need to buy disability insurance, consider a longer waiting period to reduce the cost of the premium. The waiting period is the time you have to wait after becoming ill to start receiving the benefit. Disability may arise from medical conditions or an accident; therefore, your health status is not the only factor to consider when deciding to protect yourself against long-term disability. You should consider a minimum of three months waiting period as it will cut the cost substantially.

OTHER INSURANGE

It is good to become risk conscious, however, don't allow yourself to become insurance poor. It's too expensive to insure against any and every possible risk. Decline life and disability coverage on loans and charge cards. Don't buy mortgage insurance on your home; increase your term insurance policy—it will cost less.

NOTE: Read and re-read your policies after they are delivered to you. Be certain that you have the coverage you want and need.

Dr. Rosie Milligan

MORTGAGE/RENT

When buying a home, consider your family size only. Many people who need a two-bedroom home, will buy a three-bedroom home. I have had clients say to me, "I need another bedroom so that when my family comes to visit from out of town, they will have somewhere to stay."

An additional bedroom can increase the cost of your home by as much as $30,000. Why pay a higher note plus additional interest to provide a sleeping place for someone else for a week or so?

When guests visit, welcome them to what you have— whether it is the couch, sleeping bag, floor, etc. After all, hotel and motels are available. It's cheaper for guests to pay hotel and motel fees for a week than for you to pay an additional mortgage or rent note for thirty years.

Teach children to share rooms and be happy. They can learn to do that. If they have problems with sharing a room or bed, give them a tour of the homeless sites. Sometimes, children need an awareness orientation.

Remember, you are the parent. It's your responsibility to teach them how to live and survive through good and bad times.

Everyone who's working in the house should pay rent. Those of age who are neither working nor in school should earn their keep by doing household chores, thus freeing up the time of those who are working. If this rule is applied, you will soon find everyone in the house working and paying rent. Then and only then, should the household chores be shared equally.

ELECTRICITY

- Turn the lights off in your home when you are not using them.

- Allow only a designated amount of hours for children to watch television.

- Do not go to sleep with the TV watching you, or the radio listening to itself.

- Air conditioner—keeps steady gauge, keep doors closed when air conditioner is in use.

- Wash a full load when washing versus everybody in the house washing a few pieces at a time.

- Instead of leaving your outside lights on all night, purchase sensor lights. These lights will sensor any motion nearby and come on automatically. They shut off automatically after a few minutes. The cost is as low as $20.

- Purchase items like electric fans and heater during off-season when they are less expensive.

GAS

- Maintain thermostats below 72 degrees.

- Leave heat off in rooms that are not in use and close doors to these rooms during cold periods.

- Use an electric heater to warm up the bathroom instead of over-heating the entire house in order to have a warm bathroom.

- Dress in the bathroom where it is warm.

- Use the washer and dryer discretely; wash full loads of clothing instead of one or two pieces at a time.

- Weather-strip you windows and doors.

WATER BILL

- Repair leaky faucets and any water drippings.

- Do not let the water run while you are brushing your teeth.

- Water your lawn in the evening.

FOOD

- Shop at discount outlets such as: Coscos, SAM'S Club and stock large quantities. If you are not a member, go to one of these outlets with someone who is. Shop with a friend, buy bulk items such as: toilet tissue, Kleenex, and paper towel etc., and then split it.

- Plan a weekly menu.

- Take leftovers for lunch.

- Make a grocery list before grocery shopping and when shopping stick to your list.

- Learn ways to create a new dish from leftovers and make it taste fresh and new.

- Use coupons—you really do save. Many stores offer additional savings with double coupons, which simply means you will receive double the value of the coupon.

- Get a card from the market that you frequent, you can save big time.

- Invest in a water system rather than buying single bottles water, it's pays off in the long run.

- Recycle bottles, can, etc. Cans and bottles, you will quite surprise about how much money your recycling can turn into.

You will be amazed at how much money you can save in one year if you follow the steps. The average person spends at least $5.00 per day on lunch. Some spends $.5.00 per day on coffee. Some eat out for breakfast and lunch.

People buy bottle water, beverages etc. Let's just say for the average person who spends $5.00 per day on lunch, multiply that times 5 days a week, that's 25.00 per week, $100.00 per month and $1, 200.00 per year. This figure is doubled and tripled for some people.

AUTOMOBILE

When buying a car:

1. Check to see what the insurance cost

2. Consider repair cost

3. Tune-up cost

4. Mileage per gallon, etc.

- Have your car checked and serviced as recommended. Check for comparison prices for maintenance check-ups. Sometimes, it costs more to take the car back to the dealer.

- Maintain a record book for maintenance upkeep for warranty protection. Learn to check your oil, brake fluid, power steering fluid, battery, radiator, and air in the tires. This is important because most people use self-service gas stations.

- It costs to operate an automobile! Have friends, children, and relatives pay you when you take them someplace in your car.

- Remember to carpool when possible—you will save money on gasoline and parking.

- Do not allow your gasoline tank to drop below a quarter of a tank; your car uses more gas when this occur, and this can also lead to a burned-out fuel pump

- Save on gasoline by mapping out your routes before you get started each day with errands/chores.

- Find an honest mechanic and have your car serviced. The minute you hear unusual noises or sounds, have your car checked out. Learn how to check your engine oil and change it periodically. *It's cheaper to fix a little problem before it turns into a big problem. Your car is the next largest investment after your home, and you will need a car most of your life, so treat it like an investment—watch over it and manage it well.*

- **Tips for saving at the gas pump.** (1) Slow your roll, speed eats up your fuel. Driving 5 miles over 60mph, is like paying .30 extra for every gallon of gas you burn. (2)Do not load you car down with items such as: flags, bikes, carriers, luggage, racks, etc. Excess weight makes the engine work harder, increases drag which causes wasting of fuel. Close your car window when driving at high speed, this causes drag and wasting of fuel too. (3)Be a smooth operator. Avoid jerking, frequent accelerating when trying to go around and pass other vehicles and frequent jamming on your brakes. This alone can save you $1.00 or more per gallon of gasoline---this can make a financial difference. (4)Avoid idling of your car; 15 minutes of idling can burn a quarter of a gallon of gasoline.

- **Don't be afraid to get your hands a little dirty.** Learn to check and to change your wiper blades, check belts and hoses for wear and tear, clean the dirt and dust from the engine's air-filter, the dirt and dust clogs up the filter and causes the car to use more gasoline.

- Save on gasoline by mapping out your routes before you get started each day with errands/chores.

AUTOMOBILE RELATED EXPENSES TO WATCH OUT FOR

- When driving, use a hand-free cell phone to avoid a ticket.

- Always wear your seatbelt and make sure your passenger wears a seatbelt to avoid a ticket, this could cost you $200.00 plus

- Makes sure your young child is in the proper seatbelt or boost chair according to his/her age and weight to avoid an expensive ticket.

- If you get a moving violation ticket, pay it before it cost increase, it can increase four times the original cost in a short time. Do not allow a ticket to go into a warrant.

- If you get a parking ticket, pay it before the cost increase.

- Pay your car registration fee before the fee increase, it will increase substantially.

- When parking your automobile, check the street signs posted. Do not just park without checking because you see other cars parked, this could cost you big-time for not checking for yourself.

- Where there is meter parking, it's best to put more money in the meter than what's required for the time you expect to be parked than to get a ticket—a ticket can be expensive.

- When parking in your own driveway, do not allow your vehicle to protrude onto the sidewalk, you can get a ticket.

CLOTHING

- One should go "shop looking" (also referred to as window-shopping) without any intention of buying. This exercise is to allow you to keep abreast of the cost of clothing in order to compare prices when stores are claiming a bargain sale.

- Buy off-season for real bargains (i.e. buy winter coats during the summer.) Buy fall and winter clothes when stores are clearing racks for spring and summer clothing. And, buy spring and summer clothes when stores are clearing racks for fall and winter clothes.

- Do not discard purses and shoes that can be repaired, take them to a shoe repair shop.

- Shop at Salvation Army and Good Will stores for name brand clothes. I suggest you read the book, *Thrift Store Diva: Spending Pennies and Looking Like a Million Dollars* by Helen Pearson.

CHARGE CARDS/CREDIT CARDS

- Whatever happened to lay-away and 'I'll just wait until I get the money? I have observed people paying higher prices for appliances because they were sold at a store where they accept charge cards. I have known people to pay as much as $150 more for an item in order to charge it.

- I would recommend that you leave your credit cards at home when shopping; however you cannot write a check at most places without a major credit card.

- If you carry your American Express Card, I believe that would curtail your impulsive spending, because the payment becomes due when billed.

- Pay off credit cards with the highest interest rate first or switch outstanding credit cards with a high interest to a card with a low interest rate. **Place the interest saved in a savings account.**

SCHOOL ALLOWANCE

You should check to see what lunch costs at your child's school and give him/her allowance based on facts, not on what he/said it costs. The less money they have, the easier it is to get them to eat breakfast at home.

LUNCH

Cook enough at dinner to prepare a lunch for the next day. Take salads and fruit for lunch. Buy a thermos to take juice to work instead of drinking sodas. Remember, you are what you eat and what you think. You will soon find yourself feeling better, looking better, controlling your weight better, being more productive and saving money.

NAILS

Do your own. Purchase a nail maintenance kit and do your own nails. The average woman goes to the nail shop two times per month and spending at least $25.00 per month, multiply that times twelve, you would have saved $300.00 per year at minimum.

HAIR

I won't say much about hair, but you know who you are. I am talking about people who do not wear natural hair styles. Some women are spending more than $2,000.00 per year on their hair styles and the multiple wigs for all occasions.

COSMETICS

Find a company that sells the cosmetics you like, become a distributor and purchase wholesale. The average woman spends $650.00 annually on cosmetic. If you became a distributor with a company that you liked their products, you would spend only half that much.

TELEPHONE

- Get the basic features for your telephone.

- Do not get features such as: Three-way, call forwarding, and the dial back feature unless you have reasons to use these feature at the time of installation.

- If you have relatives who are incarcerated, set limits as to how often they can call at your expense.

- If you have a cell phone, do not get a plan where you are paying for incoming calls.

- Base the minutes you purchase on the actual number of minutes you expect to use, and do not go over your allowable minutes. Going over you minutes allowed under your plan can cost you big time.

- If you do not have self control when it comes to overusing your allowable minutes, then you should get a telephone where you can buy minutes as you need them.

SPECIAL OCCASIONS

- Christmas, Birthdays, Mother's Day, Father's Day, etc.— agree as a family to just exchange a card. Learn to treat the people you love special every day and you will all save money.

- If you feel compelled to celebrate special days, then buy items when they are on sale and store them away versus buying the day or week of the occasion.

MISCELLANEOUS

Banquet tickets, raffle tickets, BBQ dinners, candy drives, and patron's lists—if the money is not in your budget for such, say, "No" and don't feel guilty!

CLUB DUES AND ASSOCIATIONS

If your budget does not permit, resign until a later date.

GARDENER

Purchase a lawn mower. Have the children do the lawn or do it yourself. The exercise will do you good.

MAGAZINES

If you do not get a chance to read on a regular basis, purchase magazine issues on an as-wanted basis.

DOCTOR AND DENTIST VISITS

Have regular check-ups as a preventive measure. It can save you many dollars. It's cheaper to have a cavity filled than a root canal.

MONTHLY PROGRESS
EVALUATION FORM

- I did all the things I said I would do to help.

- I did some of the things I said I would do to help.

- I did more than what I said I would do to help.

- I see where I can do much more to help.

List the results you can see at this point from your team effort.

List additional things you will do next month to help.

How much money did the family save from my efforts_____?

CPSIA information can be obtained
at www.ICGtesting.com
Printed in the USA
FSHW010720170920
73526FS